planet box

LAURA DALY
&
DIANA SYDER

First published in Great Britain in 2009 by Comma Press
www.commapress.co.uk

A CIP catalogue record of this book is available from the British Library

ISBN: 1-905583-24-9
EAN: 978-1-905583-24-9

The publishers gratefully acknowledge assistance from the Arts Council England
Yorkshire, as well as the support of Literature Northwest:
www.literaturenorthwest.co.uk

literaturenorthwest ◉

Set in Bembo by David Eckersall
Printed and bound in England by SRP Ltd, Exeter.

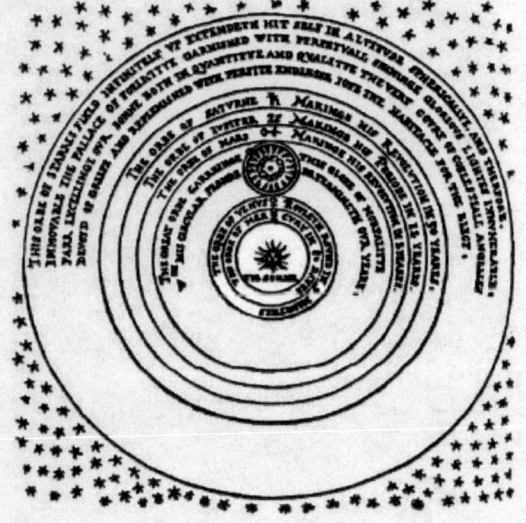

POST CARD

THE ADDRESS TO BE WRITTEN ON THIS SIDE

We are all citizens of the sky

— Camille Flammarion

The Dome

Amateur. Amo, amas, amat. He she it loves the sky
and given a pair of binoculars sees clear
to the 9th magnitude, the actual photons on her retina,
like that woodcut where a man sticks his head
through the wooden ceiling of the globe and looks outside.

It started with people giving her things she felt compelled
to honour: Nana's neighbour's postcard collection,
her father-in-law's Eighth Army medals,
then her dead ex-husband's drawings of Inner Farne
with *I am courageous* on the back in his spidery pen and ink.
Soon everyone was passing stuff on to everyone else,
bric-à-brac, school reports, symptoms
and each day was a struggle to free up surfaces.
She ran herself ragged trying to catch the details,
and that didn't include the speed of light nor how long
it would take her Subaru to circumnavigate the sun.

On a deep breath you have more molecules
of air in your lungs than there are stars
in all the galaxies in the visible universe.

She knew it. Too many coloured particles,
super-abundances of seed pods, 600 species of UK spiders,
far too many shampoos, special offers, sunshine breaks
and broken fridges, lists of friends, shoals of strangers,
thirteen digit passwords and plastic bags doubling like microbes.
Even by herself she was too many citizens.

An old couple round the corner stacked papers
to the ceiling both sides of the hall.
News lined every room and spilled on up the stairs,
as if neither dare discard a word of what'd happened
since they'd learned to read. Crazy people
but their story stuffs her in its mouth and swallows her.

3

One night, a glistening knot in the grass
had a five-toed foot where it shouldn't be.
She couldn't work it out, the likelihoods
coiling and uncoiling in her head,
till she realised this was a lizard's dream
leaking away through the coils
of a snake's dream and she woke, fighting
for breath in the stranglehold of winter.

By morning her house had gone supernova,
swollen beyond all previous orbits.
Mouse droppings in the loft were proof
everything had become a metaphor for everything else.
Come lunchtime, bookshelves buckled and external walls
bowed under the pressure of a future trying to get in.
There was no room for anything new to happen.
The whole of tomorrow was dammed to a standstill
and her breathing laboured under the press of it.

That evening the streetlight died. The silence was wonderful
and for the first time in ages she breathed easily
as if something was breathing for her or upon her or with her.
She stared at the answers brimming over her house:

everything hollow and stolen
everything forbidden or imprisoned
every different and intricate thing, every violence,
every deep and rightful thing
everything clear or simultaneous
everything coded and shining and distributed
every moment of attending or fainting.

She stepped forward.

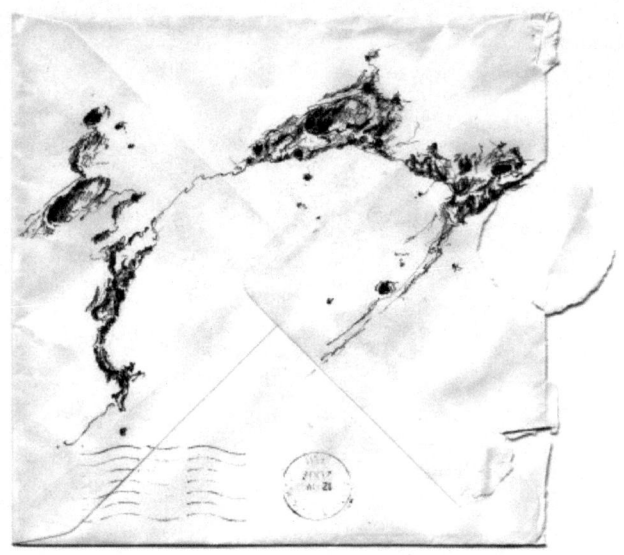

Later she joined a class, ordered a planisphere,
bought a book then several, which led to a group,
which led to binoculars, the 9th magnitude and staying up
till 3 am on the Todmorden moors for a cracking view of Mars.

There were others out on the moor who offered her
Oxo with pepper as Orion rose above the rim
of the dome and frost fur built on the roofs of the cars.
No-one showed their true shape under so many fleeces.

She worried about the man in the woodcut.
Did friends and neighbours believe him
when he told them how he'd found exactly
where earth touches the sky, fidgeted at it
with his stick till the horizon unstitched
and he could poke his head through; how he'd seen
you could question; that there is ever an answer.

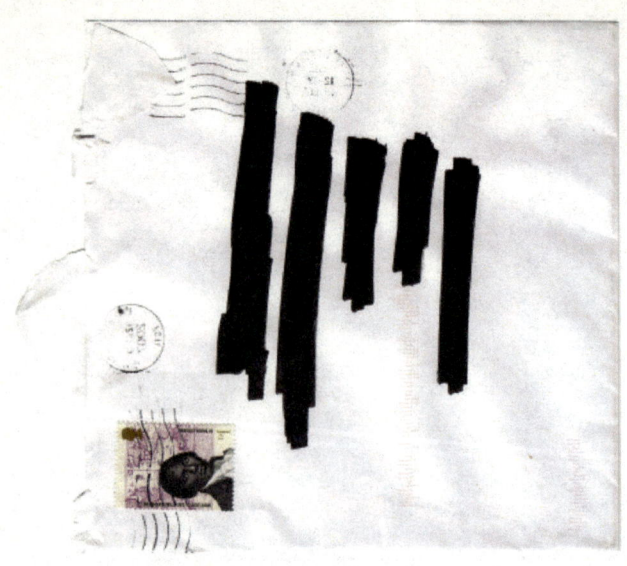

Or did they whisper, grinning, how already he'd outgrown
the curvature of the earth, bulky on all fours
and pointing like a dog at the moon?
How could they feed such a man, even at harvest?
Let him pluck the stars from their stiff stalks and eat them.

So what did the future do to him?
Strand him between the rafters, elderly and complaining?
Or did it pull him through and set him upright
looking out from the roof of his world?
He occupies her, these glittering nights up on the moors,
medieval man looking out through the sockets of her eyes
and still demanding reason from the void.

When the Telescope Comes

How they spill their hearts into her front room.
Their gravels twinkle grain upon grain.
Name settles upon name, cold to her tongue.
In the early days it's a joy. Sirius, marquise-cut,
spits fire from her finger. The Pleiades is a cluster.
Soon she has several constellations on each hand,
thinks secretly *Heaven is my oyster.*

A year of this and they fill the spare room.
She keeps records but there are too many to name.
Some stick, ring nebula F469W, but most
don't even get a number. The garage is packed.
They poke through the tarmac like weeds
and her bed floats on brilliant-cut waters.
When she scrunches to the kettle they're ankle deep
but friends stay away, leaving sharp-pointed hungers.

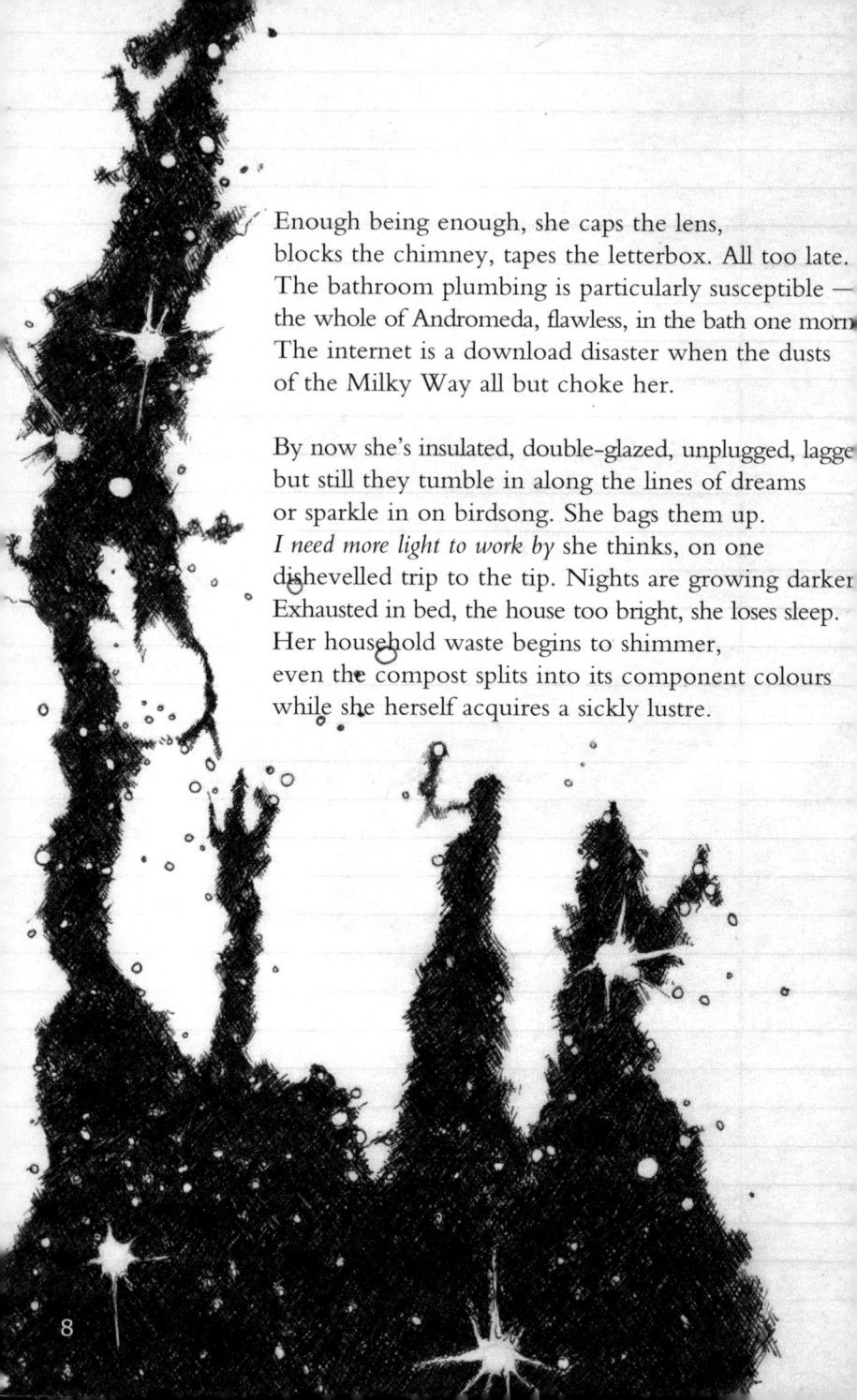

Enough being enough, she caps the lens,
blocks the chimney, tapes the letterbox. All too late.
The bathroom plumbing is particularly susceptible —
the whole of Andromeda, flawless, in the bath one morn
The internet is a download disaster when the dusts
of the Milky Way all but choke her.

By now she's insulated, double-glazed, unplugged, lagge
but still they tumble in along the lines of dreams
or sparkle in on birdsong. She bags them up.
I need more light to work by she thinks, on one
dishevelled trip to the tip. Nights are growing darker
Exhausted in bed, the house too bright, she loses sleep.
Her household waste begins to shimmer,
even the compost splits into its component colours
while she herself acquires a sickly lustre.

Where will it end? she frets, plagued by shadows.
The only way we can know things exist
is because they emit light. So is it a test,
this lit and unlit room, to discern
one flickering human picture against a ceiling
of unremitting splendour? If so, how to answer?

She skims the ads for alternative lenses:
one promises to slip the world faster than ever
through her fingers; another guarantees
such a perfect fit the world settles down,
soft-focussed, easy, but the third sets her heart racing,
for when an object is placed at its focus,
light leaves the lens in parallel lines,
the image, therefore, carried far into space.
With a smooth double action. At a new, lower price.

What a simple, elegant, storage solution.
She sees herself flitting between planets as they rise and set,
dispersing her selves with all their belongings
through so many spare rooms, with so much scope
for safe-keeping and correlations across the field of view.

She writes a cheque, relieved everything
will soon be stowed quite near to hand,
while being out of mind and out of sight.
It will take time. Virtual travel will have its snags
but when it's done, she'll log on to the umbilical thoughts
of others who've flown, every view finally falling
back to earth with its cloud cover
and storms always flickering somewhere.

And under that weather of the future
a woman will close the curtains of a simple room
where there is firelight, enough lamplight to read by.
In a lifelong discipline of lenses, time has restored
each star to its place and she has become
so effortless and smooth, so accurate and clear
that in the end, nothing has been wasted.

HOTEL BAD SCHACHEN

A gate slams in the wind that gusts
from wherever it came from before she was born
and mice, who still gnaw on shadows,
hear it sing under the door, lift the rug's fringe
and enter the thicket of the woman's bones
till, out through her mouth, it passes on.
Or was it light? Or was it life?

The room is spacious, airy, clean.

MERCURY

Max distance from sun	69.7
Min distance from sun	45.9
	(millions of km)
Orbital period (earth days)	87.97
Rotation period (earth days)	58.64
Orbital inclination	7°
Axial inclination	2°
Mass (earth = 1)	0.055
Volume (earth = 1)	0.056
Density (water = 1)	5.44
Surface gravity (earth = 1)	0.38
Average surface temp.	+167 °C
Albedo (fraction of light it reflects)	0.11
Equatorial diameter	4,878 km
Number of moons	0

NB – temp varies between 350°C in the day to –33°C at night.

$$1 \text{ parsec} = 3.2616 \text{ light years} =$$
$$2.065 \times 10^5 \text{ AU} =$$
$$3.857 \times 10^{13} \text{ Km}$$

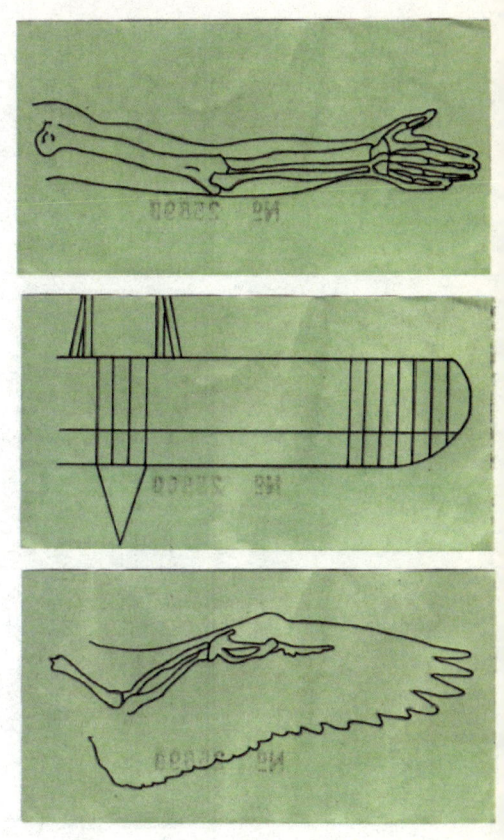

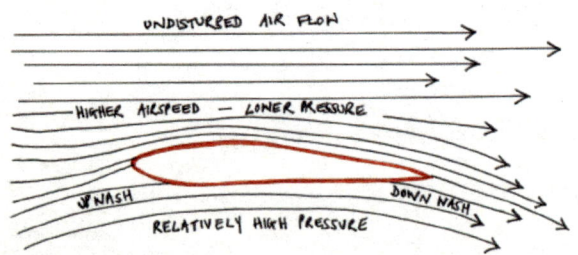

	M	J	Sat	u	N	P
24.9	816	1507	3004	4537		7375
206.7	741	1347	2735	4456	4425	
·3d	687 d	11.86 y	27.46 y	84.01 y	164.84 y	247.74
6m 04s	24h 37m 23s	9h55m30s	10h13m59s	17h 14m	16h 7m	6d 9h 17s
	1.8	1.3	2.5	0.8	1.8	17.15
·4	24.0	3.0	26.4	98	28.8	122.5
	0.11	317.9	95.2	14.6	17.2	0.002
2	3.94	1.33	0.71	1.27	1.77	2.02
	0.38	2.64	1.16	1.17	1.2	0.06
	−65	−110	−140	−195	−200	−225
37	0.15	0.52	0.47	0.51	0.41	0.6
756	6794	143,884	120,536	51,118	50,538	232k
1	2	61	33	26	13	1
1	0.15	1319	744	67	57	0.01

Eris.
Jupiter Bell.

	M	V
dist. from sun { max (millions of km) { min	69.7 / 45.9	109 / 107.4
orbital period (? earth days)	87.97 d	224.7
rotation period	58.646 d	243.16 d
orbital inclination ° (deg)	7.0	3.4
axial inclination ° deg	2	178
mass (earth = 1)	0.055	0.815
density (water = 1)	5.44	5.25
surface gravity (Earth = 1)	0.38	0.90
ave surface temp °C	+167	+464
albedo = fract. of light it reflects	0.11	0.65
diameter, km (equatorial)	4878	12,104
number of moons	0	0
volume Earth = 1	0.056	0.8

from Philip's Night Sky Atlas

Philip's : Robin Scagell   2004, ho
(except Eris, m

20

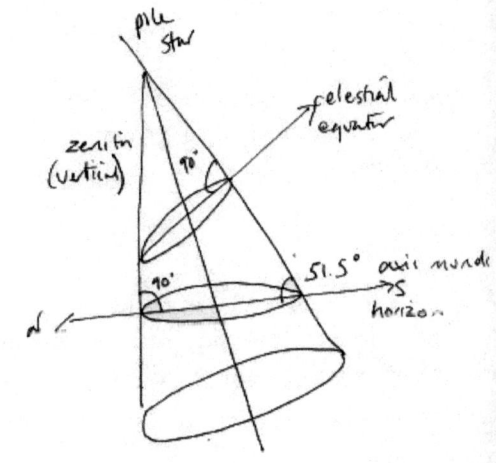

pole
star

celestial
equator

zenith
(vertical)

90°

90°

51.5° axis mundi
→S
horizon

N ←

CONIC GEOMETRIES

Mercury

On the dark side, gravels of herself before she can remember
are laid across a speechless plain, almost no atmosphere,
with all its volatiles lost to space, till language rescues her
and gives her words to breathe.

With practice she learns

and a first memory stalls on the shadow rim — Aunty Mary's biscuit tin,
with whole ones in silver paper. *Do you want another, pet?*
No thankyou. She could say *Yes.* But her mother watches.

Lightweight impacts that spin

her into cataracts of daylight and the scalding heat
of dancing, arms wide, as if she might link any two opposites
because giving and receiving are one. Such a small planet, moving so fast

All's empty space

and making toffee apples. Milk teeth and sticky arguments that burn and set.
The reek of it fills the house and splinters the surface of Sundays.
daddy says he's sorry, mummy, and *mummy wants to be friends now, daddy.*

Slabs of greediness and lies.

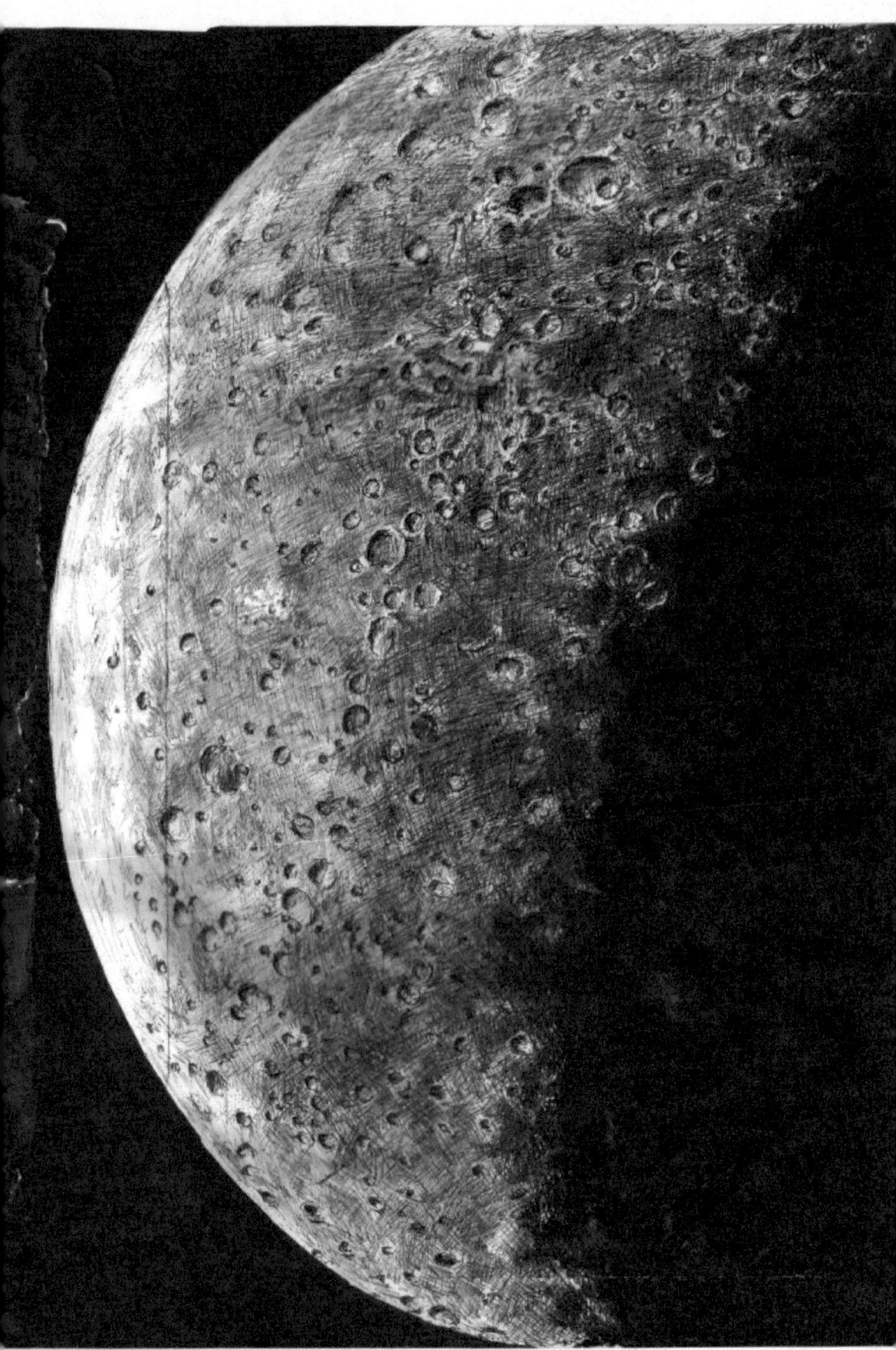

VENUS

Max distance from sun	109
Min distance from sun	107.4
	(millions of km)
Orbital period (earth days)	224.7
Rotation period (earth days)	243.16
Orbital inclination	3.4°
Axial inclination	178°
Mass (earth = 1)	0.815
Volume (earth = 1)	0.86
Density (water = 1)	5.25
Surface gravity (earth = 1)	0.90
Average surface temp.	+464 °C
Albedo (fraction of light it reflects)	0.65
Equatorial diameter	12,104 km
Number of moons	0

it has 167 volcanoes bigger
than 100km across (earth only has one)

Venus

On Venus, days are longer than its year
so she's chosen the lava plains round Maxwell Montes
to stock-pile those slow-release raptures that sustain her:
archery and the science of accuracy; libraries;
also the pure concentrations of drawing and dance
that are the nearest she gets to thought without language.

This world melts her shoes, burns her off
in the heat of the day when lightning kicks in
and every nerve splays to the perimeter.
At best she siphons off its energies, at worst
measures ordinary days against red letter ones
when seismic forces bubble up into twists of fate.
Meanwhile, sheer stacks of love and friendship
are gifts and tricks from the cooling lava.

It's a heat trap that raises her game
and blacksmiths in her family tree could explain
a need for magnetic storms or sparks in the throat.
It might account for the grit in her eye.
Look - there goes the phoenix.
His song's a plume of black ash that opens
up a lead through thirty kilometres of atmosphere.

Tin and lead are molten here but no heat source
is to be trusted and she checks daily for signs
of cooling because she wouldn't know where
to look for alternative sources of fuel.
So it's vital to enter new dreams while ever the metal runs,
because sometimes there are glimpses
of a shabby room with long and useless days to fill,
where there's no more she could bear to learn or possess
and everything lies belly up in the dust, with nothing
to grow young again or risk losing its wings for.

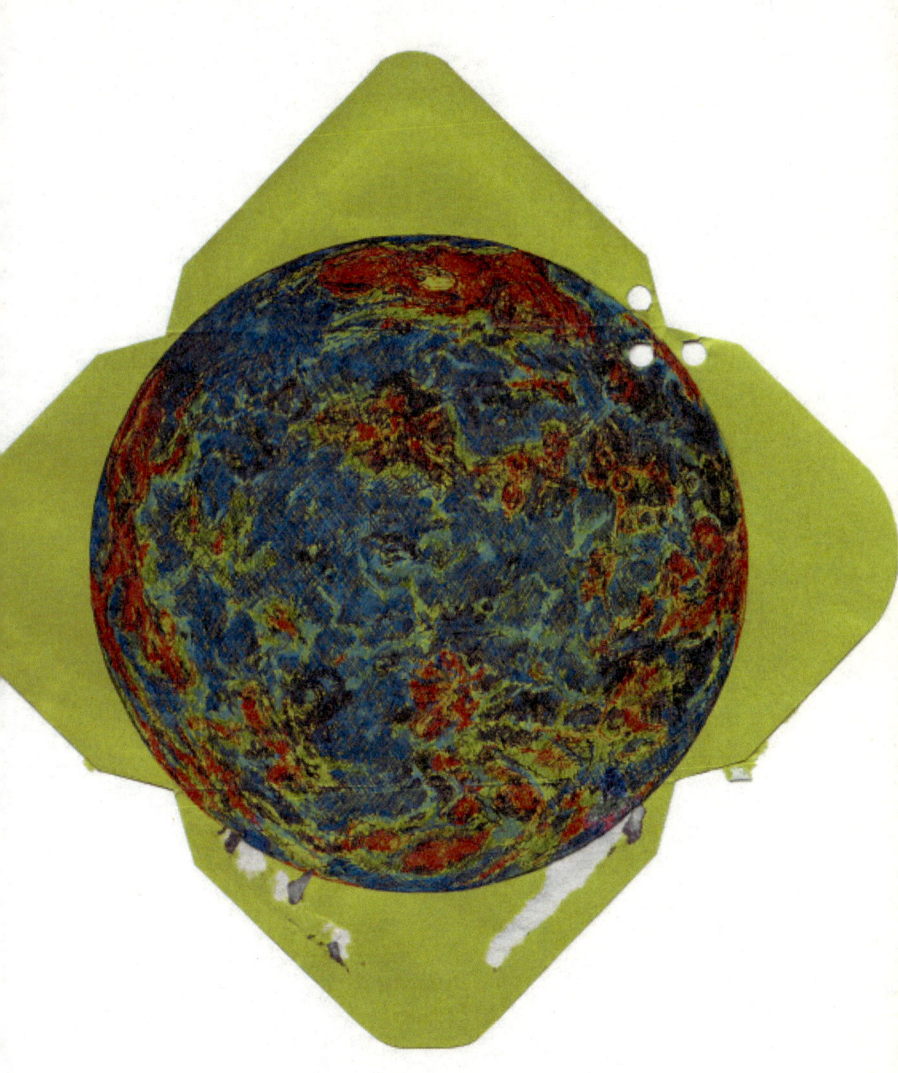

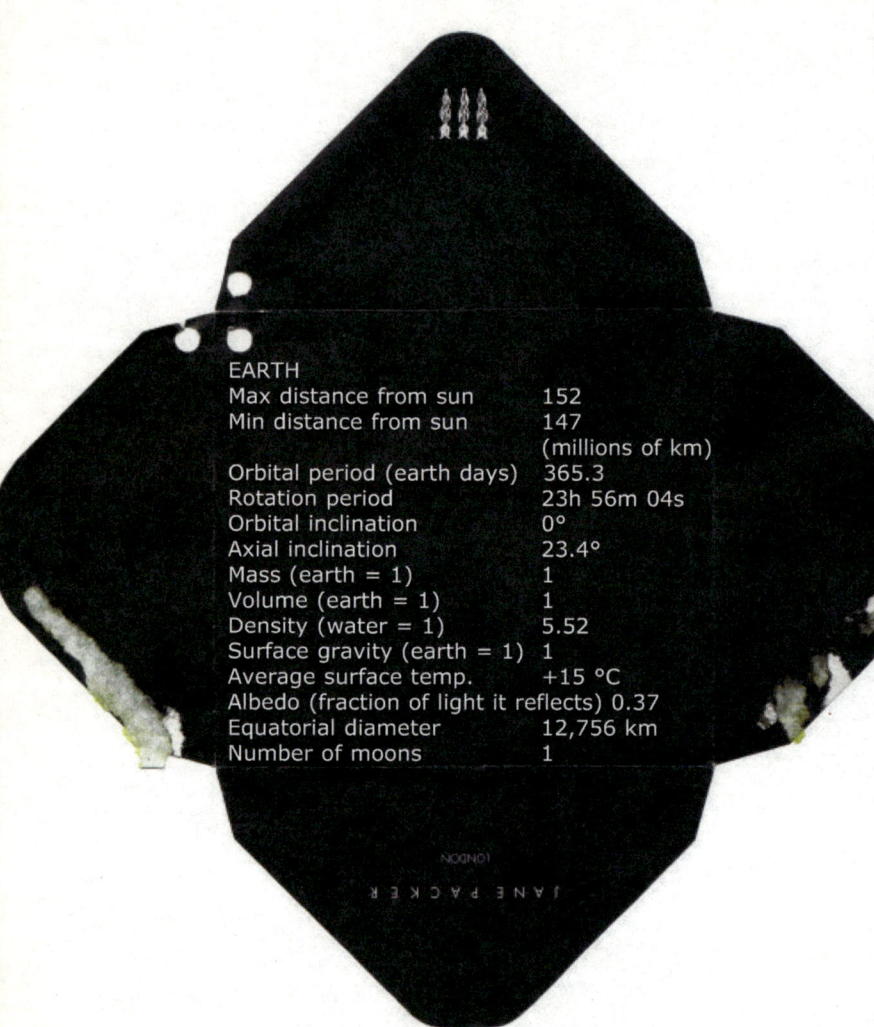

Earth

Morning Glory in a ditch; Stitchwort;
that in any talk about individual leaves,
the ratio of length to width is crucial;

earth ground through the inner velvets
of a worm; murder in the night;
a new pattern in the world, breathing

                    as if it were enough.

The structure of glycine; why
80% of bluetits must die, imagining the sky
thick with them, that Nature is wasteful;

ion pumps and counter-current exchanges;
knowing the energy released
by a snowflake if it fell onto the moon

                    as if it were enough.

An hour's drive to the power station,
the city centre, the landfill site;
a bare bulb in a tin room;

the Angel of the North above fields of rape;
being neither snake nor apple - different
ways to go on living in the world

                    as if it were enough.

A footstep and a thousand mile walk;
the circle and the spiral and the line;
accents that change along the journey;

she catches the train to Newcastle,
always adding herself to the beauty,
always wanting more

                    as if it were enough.

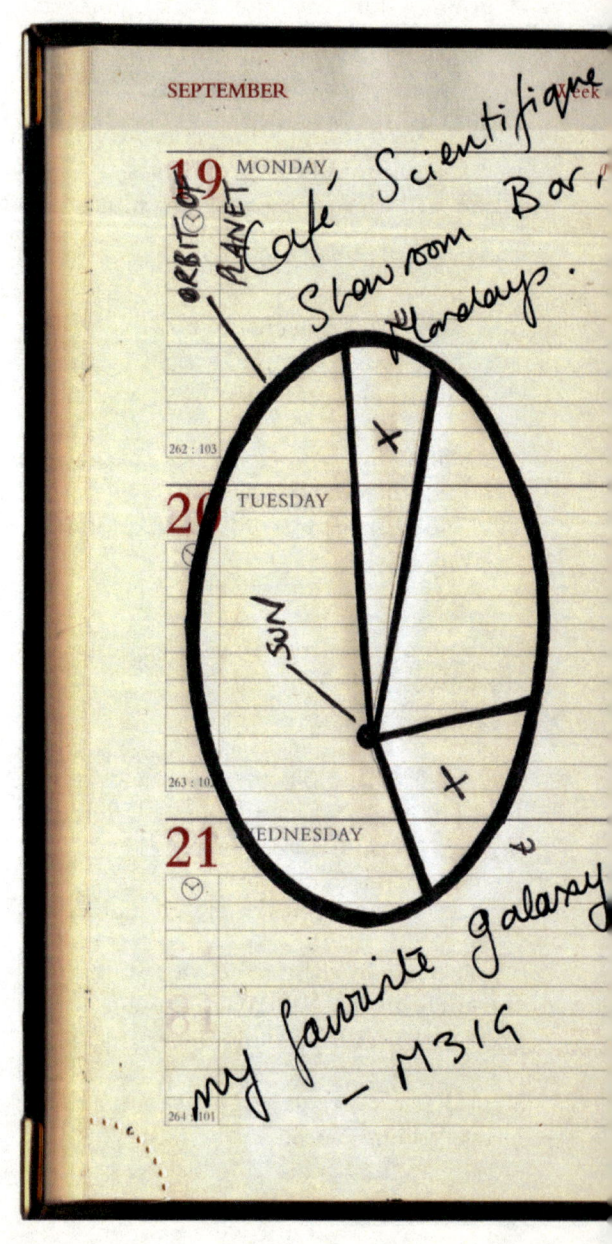

19 MONDAY

ORBIT
PLANET

Café Scientifique

Showroom Bar,

Mondays.

262 : 103

20 TUESDAY

SUN

263 : 10

21 WEDNESDAY

my favourite galaxy

– M31G

264 101

owmen of the Peak —

THURSDAY **22**

al Equinox — Autumn begins (Northern Hemisphere)

AGM minutes by

Thursday .

ORBITAL
PERIOD
/ = S

5 : 100

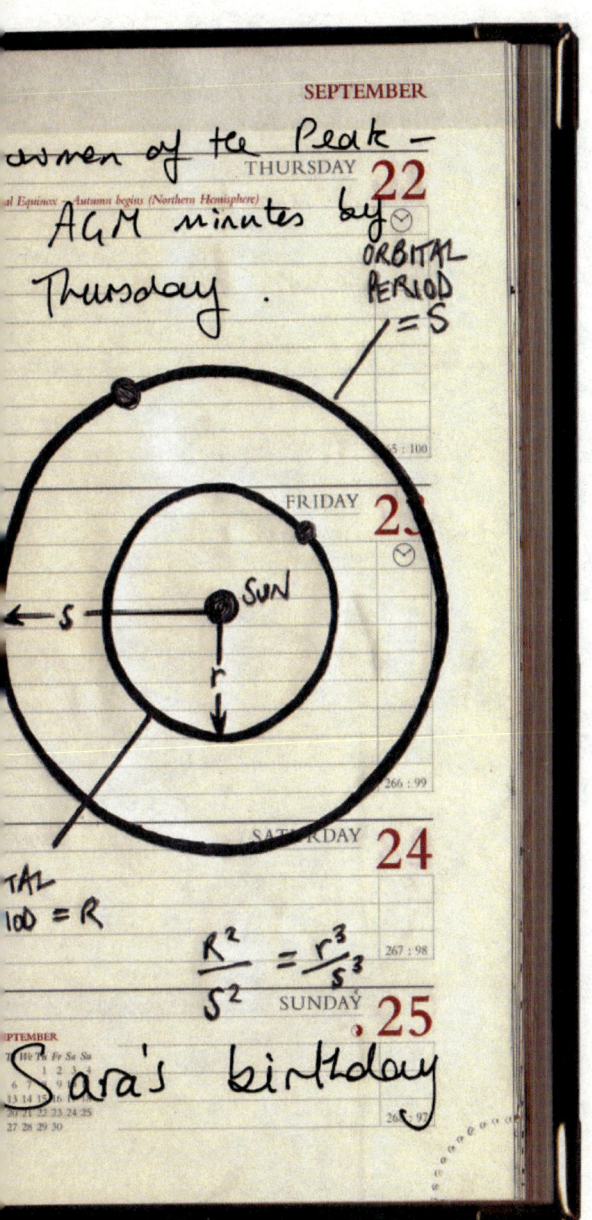

FRIDAY **23**

SUN

← S

r

266 : 99

SATURDAY **24**

TAL
100 = R

$$\frac{R^2}{S^2} = \frac{r^3}{s^3}$$

267 : 98

SUNDAY **25**

SEPTEMBER
M Tu We Th Fr Sa Su
        1 2 3 4
5 6 7 8 9 10 11
13 14 15 16
20 21 22 23 24 25
27 28 29 30

Sara's birthday

26 : 97

31

10 MONDAY   (USA-CAN.)

283 : 82

11 TUESDAY

284 : 81

12 WEDNESDAY

285 : 80

THURSDAY 13

286 : 79

FRIDAY 14

287 : 78

SATURDAY 15

288 : 77

SUNDAY 16

289 : 76

33

MOON

Orbital period	27.3 days
Rotation period seen from sun	29.4 days
Mean orbital velocity	7.89 km/s
Velocity	30km/s

- lunar soil contains 3 minerals
  not found on earth.

- there is no carbon!

- 382 kg of moon rock has been
  brought back to earth

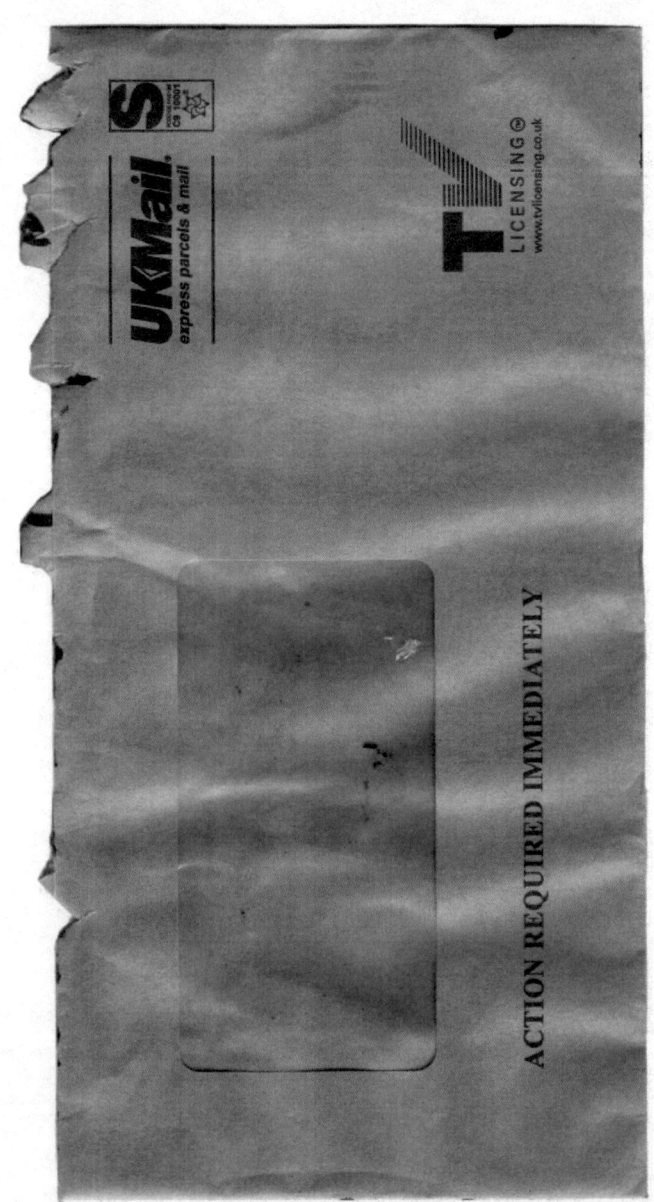

ACTION REQUIRED IMMEDIATELY

Moon

A footprint in moon dust stays sharp for millions of years,
so she builds a house in the Bay of Rainbows
to safeguard the gifts this world has delivered:

she's going to be Mary, but her mother, in labour,
spies through the taxi window the full blossom of the moon.
Odd how she's always had her mother in that taxi
on her own, but now she wants her father in there too,
both struck and making promises, anything,
re-naming their eager child *Diana*, if it's alright,
if it's a girl, as near as they can hope to get
to giving her the moon, or giving something to it;

Bra. & Bingley

PO Box No. 88, Croft Road, Crossflatts, Bingley, West Yorkshire BD16 2UA.

nineteen. Coming up on deck at 4 am alone.
A flat calm dawn. Aegean islands for the first time.
There's never been a sea so silky, rippling
from the ferry bow, such a desiccated moonskin.
There's never been a boat, yet overnight
she's sailed into the wide-open, rosy, world,
wants to run and run and run with the joy of it;

midnight. Draughts rattle an open window.
Thunder undermines the house, splits light from dark,
reveals the owl from her barn on the bedstead,
eye to eye and the sky crackling with connections.
Three times silhouetted then he's gone.
Next morning, moonshit on the bed post;

after archery there's a full moon with the biggest halo ever.
Saint Moon in a soapy hole that's spread apart the oil-slick night.
Just four hundred thousand kilometres from earth, or a three second
round-trip for the laser pulse of her heart's longing. She sights
at the bull's eye, plots trajectories, gets maximum points, thinks
People have walked there. That's creepy.

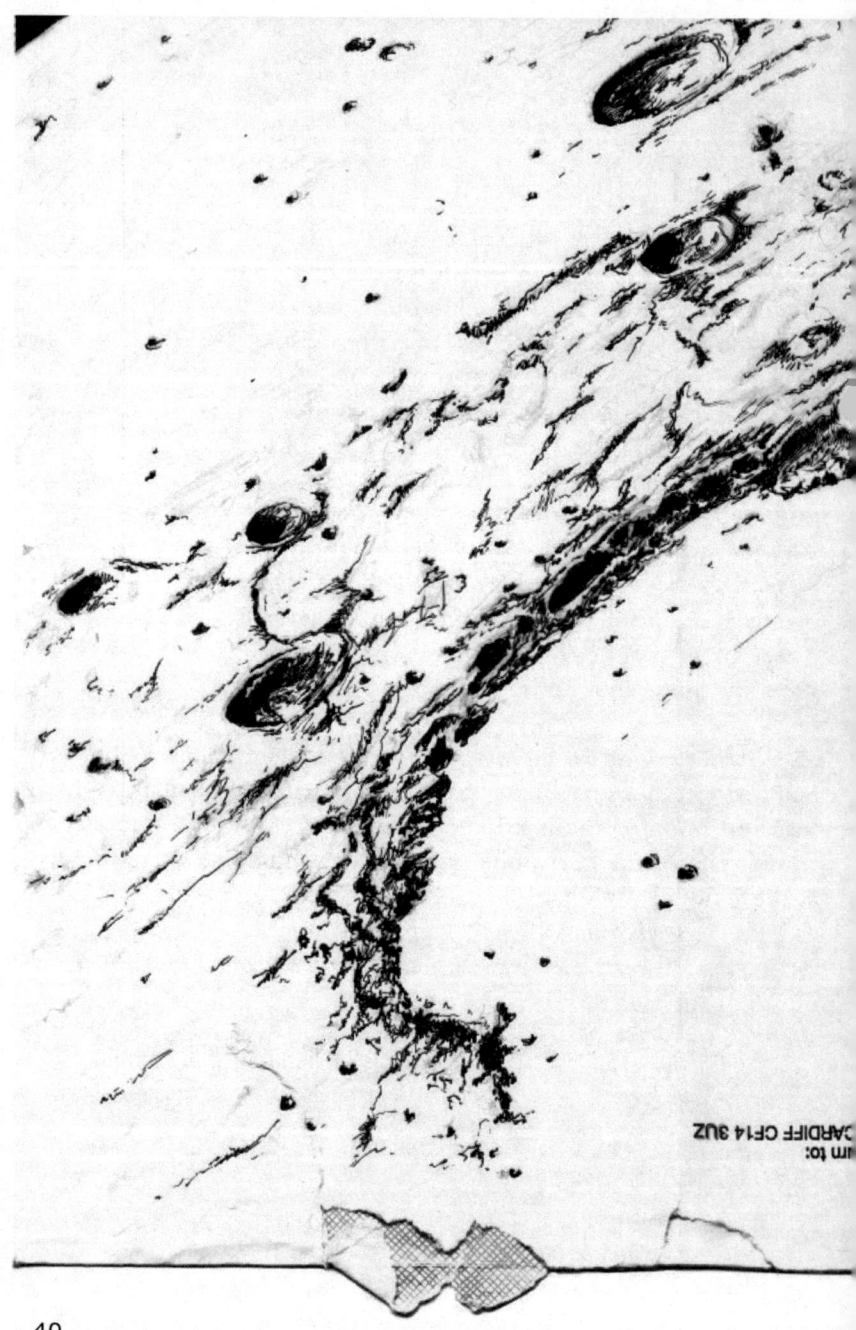

40

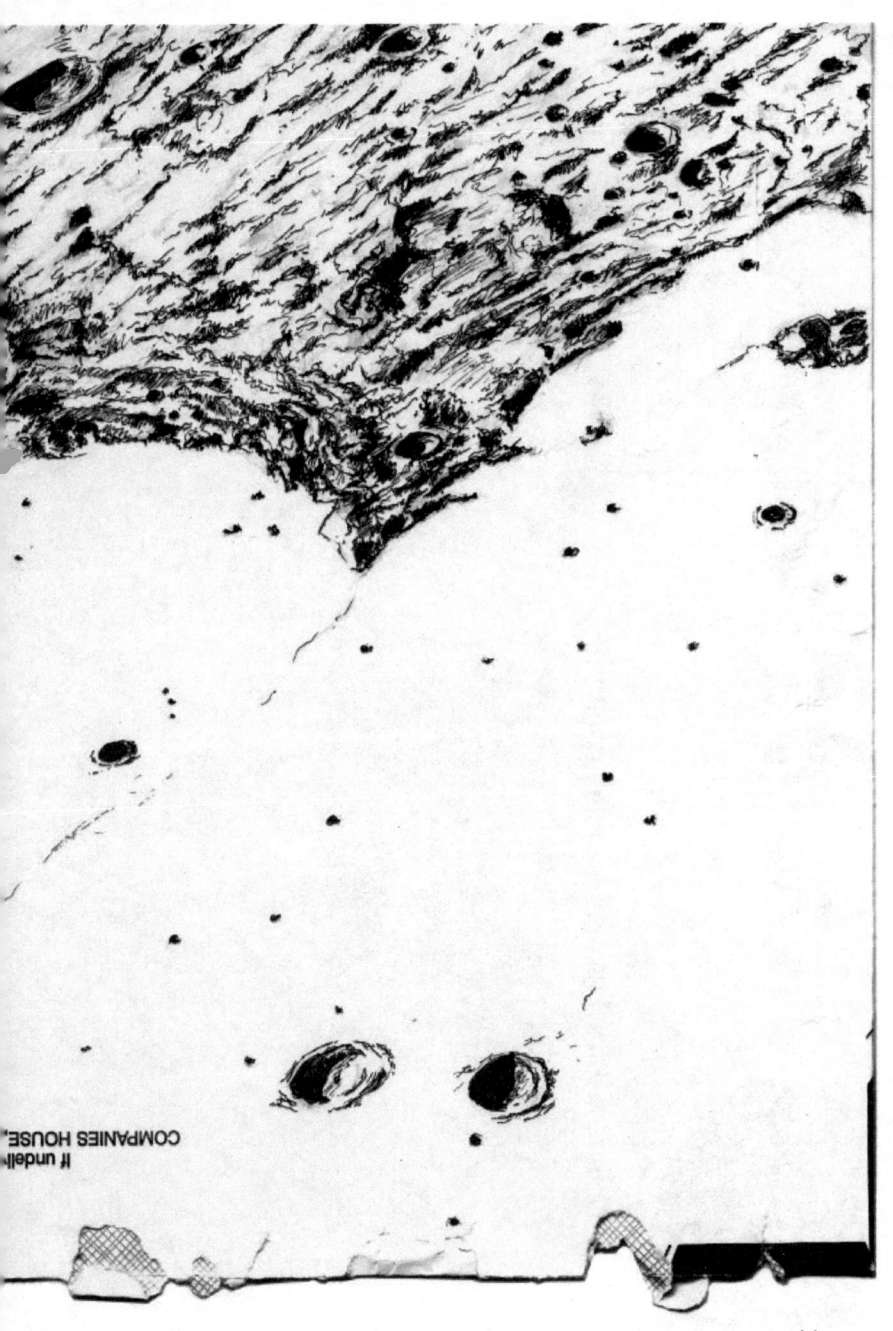

41

On Her Majesty's Service

ROYAL MAIL

2

POSTAGE PAID GB
PHQ316

Companies House
— for the record —

Annual Return Enclosed - Action Required

Deadline

MARS

Max distance from sun	24.9
Min distance from sun	206.7
	(millions of km)
Orbital period (earth days)	687
Rotation period	24h 37m 23s
Orbital inclination (deg)	1.8°
Axial inclination (deg)	24°
Mass (earth = 1)	0.11
Volume (earth = 1)	0.15
Density (water = 1)	3.94
Surface gravity (earth = 1)	0.38
Average surface temp.	-65 °C
Albedo (fraction of light it reflects)	0.15
Equatorial diameter	6,794 km
Number of moons	2

Olympus Mons = 3 × the height of Everest.

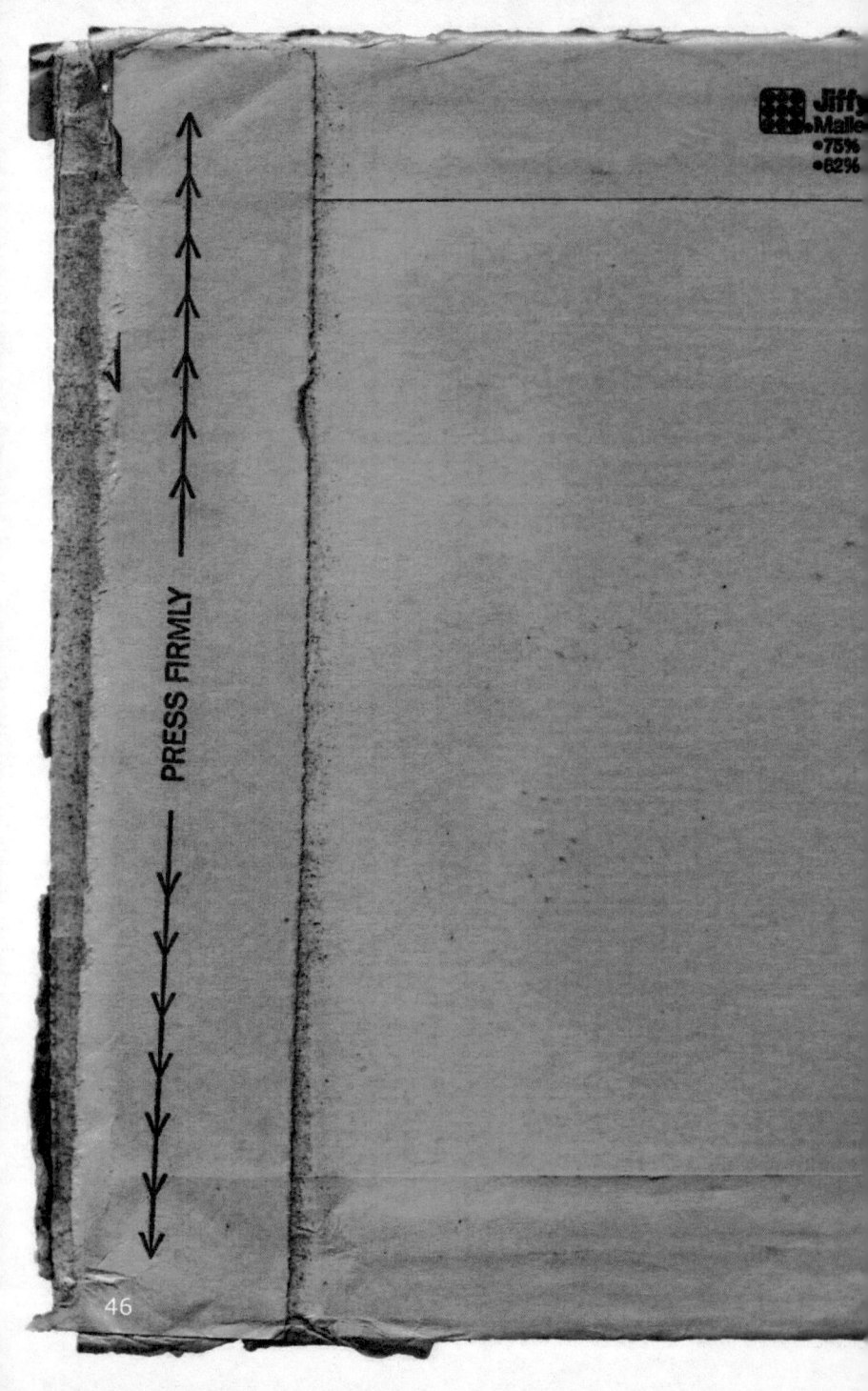

PRESS FIRMLY

Mars

It's taken months to cut and glue the jigsaw,
the entire Martian surface, frame by frame.
Now she draws boundaries with a ruler,
highlights the morning and evening mountains,
keeps weather notes: *winds light to variable*
with occasional scattered high cloud.

Here will be a village and, here, the road from a to b.
This is a field or where a field will stand if ever grass grows.
From its margin the real march begins. She sees frost
for the first time on the northern plains and builds a box to stand on.
I have a right to clean air, she declares, in a choking atmosphere.

I have a right to a clean floor, as she sweeps the everlasting dust.
To peace of mind, shouted across an empty plain. *Freedom.*

She nocks an arrow. Wherever it lands, a house.
The empty quarter will accommodate the graves
of unknown travellers and tended close beside,
a memorial to points of view will be polished
by the sun on days that dawn glittering and cold.
The native language, quaintly, will have extra words
to occupy the subtle territories between enemy and friend.

But is her own house big enough?
Her selfishness is a long, thin solitude under the sky.
Why not pencil in a pipeline, sign a mineral deal?
Just when she'd thought there was nothing more
she needed to possess, it seems her rich man
and her poor man still have plenty to discuss.

Even so, this planet's not War. It's not Astronomy,
nor Science, though it's found in astronomy books
and scientists are returning with their Buggys and Mars Rovers.
It's another room, a stony garden over the road.
On this spot she'll rig the hammock and while bees
fizz in sunlight above fallen, fermenting pears,
she'll shut her eyes and decide how much
she wants to live here, whether she could
learn a new language and be capable
of hating or hurting in order to keep it,
whether anything is, deeply, worth dying for?

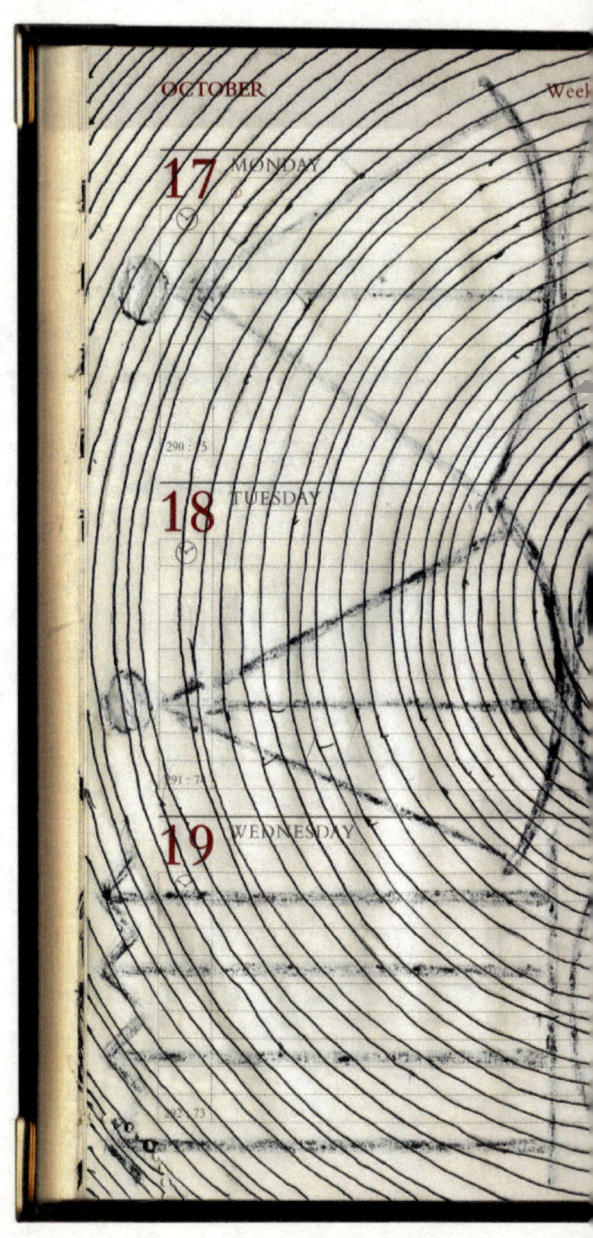

THURSDAY 20

FRIDAY 21

SATURDAY 22

SUNDAY 23

OCTOBER
Mo Tu We Th Fr Sa Su
              1 2
3 4 5 6 7 8 9
10 11 12 13 14 15 16
17 18 19 20 21 22 23
24 25 26 27 28 29 30
31

JUPITER

Max distance from sun	816
Min distance from sun	741
	(millions of km)
Orbital period (earth years)	11,86
Rotation period	9h 55m 30s
Orbital inclination	1.3°
Axial inclination	3.0°
Mass (earth = 1)	317.9
Volume (earth = 1)	1319
Density (water = 1)	1.33
Surface gravity (earth = 1)	2.64
Average surface temp.	-110 °C
Albedo (fraction of light it reflects)	0.52
Equatorial diameter	143,884 km
Number of moons	61

✳ rotation period is 9hrs 50 mins + 30 secs,
despite its mul greater diameter than
earth; rotation speed velocity is
22,000 mph (earth spins at 1000 mph
at equator) AND SO — Jupiter visibly
bulges at its equator

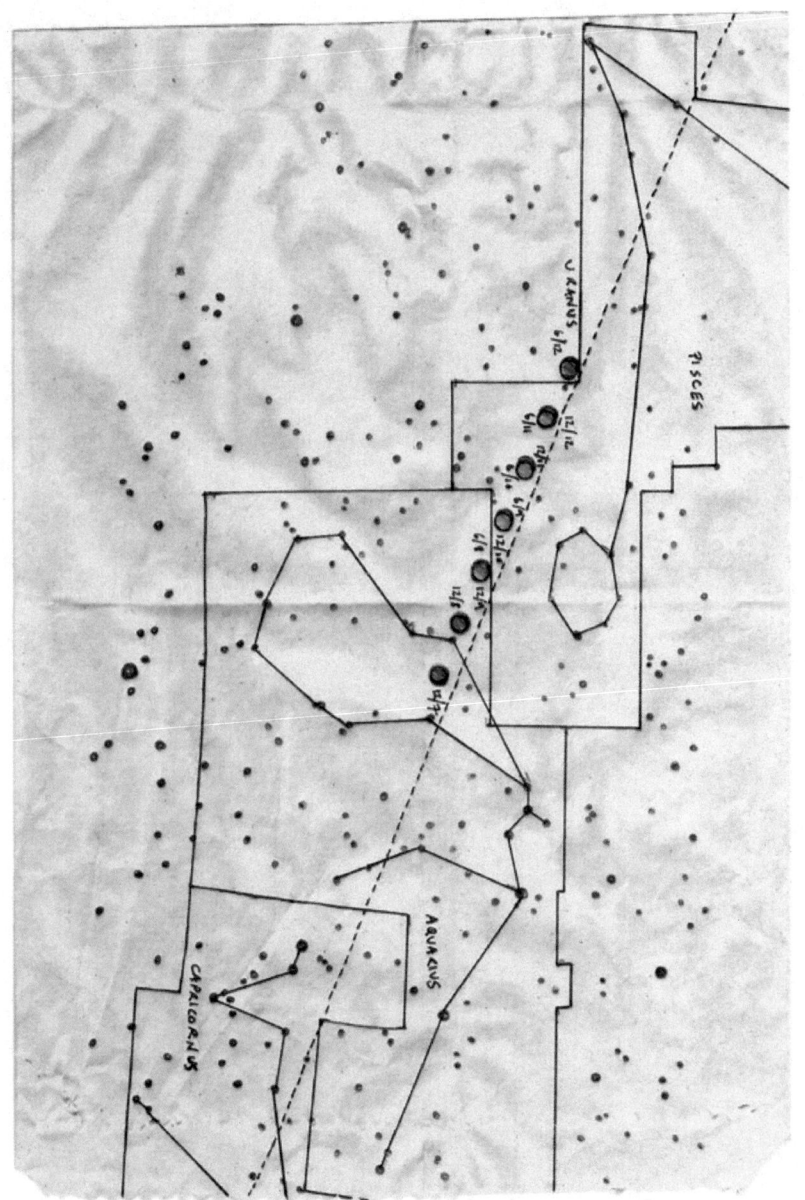

Jupiter

She started a record of Monday mornings,
dental appointments in the rain, queues into Sheffield
then turning up for work and getting it over with,
at some point a coffee but even that not how she likes it.
Later, visiting her mother when she doesn't want to,
cooking tea when she'd rather not.

Days when the postman misses her house out
are included, as are afternoons willing the phone
to liven things up, while mice eat their way through
the phone book in the cupboard and the silence of thousands
is a shadowy nest for draughts to flow through.

There are tickets from standstill days
on the train, the plane, the bus.
Also crinkle-edged photos from shades of grey days:
fourteen in this one, the cat in her arms looks cross.
Neither of them wanted to be there, furious, helpless.
Her hair is too bushy. Its fur was hot and smelled
of heatwave and the fumes off next door's vinegar vats.
This cat, although loved, was only a cat and restless.
She and it cancel each other out, so what's volatile here
is sour heat bounced from the redbrick, fur that hurts to touch.

She even keeps small change from house-bound days
when she longs to convert one letter to a horse and gallop away
instead of sweeping grit and bits from under the sofa,
cleaning the same old mould in the same old damp corner.
What if she gets asthma? What if she doesn't?

Much of her life's worn out this way
but still it mounts up silent as pollen on the bee's back.
She'll never figure the full freight of what she's started,
those trailing streamers of cause and effect,
but she knows that no-one in the world is harmless.

This house looks shoddy in daylight, yet glows
in the quiet of a day safely lived through to a lit fire,
curtains drawn, tea on the go, or in a twilight
when pigeons call from all the ancient openings
of a town, the felt of it muffling the ground
and sounding a baffled bell in the brain, which sleeps.

This then, is the bulk of her, what she is doing
with her three wishes, on a half-empty, half-full planet.

SATURN

Max distance from sun	1507
Min distance from sun	1347
	(millions of km)
Orbital period (earth years)	29.46
Rotation period	10h 13m 59s
Orbital inclination	2.5°
Axial inclination	26.4°
Mass (earth = 1)	95.2
Volume (earth = 1)	744
Density (water = 1)	0.71
Surface gravity (earth = 1)	1.16
Average surface temp.	-140 °C
Albedo (fraction of light it reflects)	0.47
Equatorial diameter	120,536 km
Number of moons	33

!!! would float in water! (handwritten annotation)

56

Patent GB 2316670

Saturn

She's suspicious of light years, astronomical units,
because nothing is yet proven about the orbit
of Saturn measured in tiredness, the radii of its rings
as a function of astonishment, or the distance
from Sirius rounded up to the nearest joy.

So she starts working out her own height in parsecs
but the calculator ejects the decimal place
into a parallel universe, three times.
On paper her mind won't hold one rope of figures
while she imports the next, but with patience it turns out
her neighbour is 1 gigasecond old, and her best friend
will be 2 thousand million seconds come November.

Human beings, she reads, *sit half way between
the biggest and the smallest things on earth.*
But how can she ever be the proper size,
seeming alternately the most abundant element
in the universe or less than a pollen grain?
Nothing's fixed, especially when she finds out
Saturn would float in water

and especially when none of this balancing stopped
her own sibling moon shattering into a billion doubts.
How they argued. How they smashed and circle now
in independent orbit, paradoxes nested one inside the other.
Under all those shining silences, what's right?
Inside all the rings of hurting, what's safe?
She thinks nothing and nothing ever can be.
Her kind heart and her greedy heart are separate satellites,
bright ice ornaments between which the static builds.

Wooden-hearted she wonders whether to work
for charity and help humanity or to clear her own track,
felling trees (or the last statues of the last trees),
all breach and vibrations, from the shaken stone.
In these woods she has started walking,
unsure which units to use for plotting distance.
Number of footsteps? Calories burned?
None seems deep or broad enough to count
for every soil spot, spider's web, struggling seed.

And whatever the scale, no matter how many
fir cones she brings home, in the end she must leave
the walk to endure the night in its own way, like it did
before anyone guessed the names of walks or parts of walks.
Incidentally, if a walk swallowed her would anyone know?
Would they remember she'd a name of her own once?

But how can she claim any proper noun while names come and go?
Certainly not yet, not on this lightweight, gas-giant world
where everything wafts and dribbles and seeps
till there's no such stuff as footprint, web, cone.
Her stomach churns. Then it happens again.
She defines something as simple
as her own skin and separates from cloud,
heavier than Saturn, and in the same breath, falling.

61

URANUS

Max distance from sun	3004
Min distance from sun	2735
	(millions of km)
Orbital period (earth years)	84.01
Rotation period	17h 14m
Orbital inclination	0.8°
Axial inclination	98°
Mass (earth = 1)	14.6
Volume (earth = 1)	67
Density (water = 1)	1.27
Surface gravity (earth = 1)	1.17
Average surface temp.	-195 °C
Albedo (fraction of light it reflects)	0.51
Equatorial diameter (km)	51,118
Number of moons	26

because its axis is horizontal
it rolls round the sun on its rim

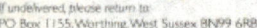

Cancer Screening Programmes

NHS

516060

Do you need to pay prescription charges? Read all the statements in Part 1 opposite. You don't have to pay a prescription charge if one (or more) of the exemptions applies to you (the patient) on the day you are asked to pay. Put a cross in the first Part 1 box that applies to you, read the declaration and complete and sign **Part 3**.

Pension Credit guarantee credit (PCGC) replaced Minimum Income Guarantee (MIG) in October 2003. If you get PCGC tick "aged 60 or over" – line C. If you (the patient) are a partner aged under 60 of someone getting PCGC tick "S – has a partner who gets Pension Credit guarantee credit". Pension Credit **savings** credit on its own does not entitle you to help.

Proof. Show the person dispensing your prescription valid proof of why you don't have to pay, such as a benefit book, exemption or pre-payment certificate. If you cannot show proof, you can still get your medicine free, but the NHS Counter Fraud and Security Management Service (NHS CFSMS) are more likely to check your entitlement later if you do not show proof.

Paying Prescription charges? You (or your representative) should put in Part 2 the amount you have paid and then sign and complete **Part 3.**

Want help with prescription charges? You can get information by ringing 0845 850 1166 or by reading leaflet HC11. You may be able to get an HC11 from your surgery or pharmacy. Or, ring 08701 555 455 to get one. Or go to www.dh.gov.uk and enter "HC11" in the search facility.

Not entitled to free prescriptions? Pre-pay. You may find it cheaper to buy a pre-payment certificate (PPC) if you think you will have to get more than 5 items in 4 months or 14 items in 12 months. Phone 0845 850 0030 to find out the cost, or order a PPC and pay by credit or debit card. Buy on-line at www.ppa.org.uk. By cheque – get an application form (FP95) from your pharmacy or go to www.dh.gov.uk and enter "Prepayment" in the search facility – the FP95 tells you what to do.

Unsure whether you should pay? You should pay for this prescription and ask for a receipt form FP57. You must get a receipt when you pay the charge, you cannot get one later. If you find you didn't have to pay, you can claim your money back up to 3 months after paying. The FP57 tells you what to do.

Information about the medicine or other items on this form will be processed centrally to pay monies due to the pharmacist, doctor or appliance contractor for items they have supplied to you. The NHS will also use this information to analyse what has been prescribed and the cost. The NHS CFSMS may use information from this form to prevent and detect fraud and incorrectness in the NHS.

Penalty Charges. If you are found to have made a wrongful claim for free prescriptions, you will face penalty charges and may be prosecuted under powers introduced by the Health Act 1999. Routine checks are carried out on exemption claims including some where proof may have been shown. You may be contacted in the course of such checks.

t.

ialist radiologist his letter within

ical problem and

w small changes, t for Chesterfield

s.

loyal Hospital.

e to be screened to ask for an

ents or suggestions areas.

spital **NHS**

on Trust
246 277271

BScAppt02

Uranus

Uranus spins her on the negative, bowls her along
out of kilter at the news of someone else's catastrophe
and she comes to in a toppled over world
of lives left as road-kill on hit and run days.

Nothing accumulates here but trepidation.
It snags on inspiration like a pulled rib
as backache spreads nearer and nearer the brain.
                          What to hold on to?

She wonders if knowledge protects
against aneurysms, strokes and neurological diseases.
Whether it can be prophylactic against malaria's thready pulse,
against *Help me*, from the open door of the side ward,
against jagged pinnacles of toothache, against past and future wars.
                          This experiment is a failure.

To begin with she trusts the great panacea
in which Love is the father, mother, brother, sister
but the animals start dying, the great trees fail.
Sometimes part of the universe loves her —
the warm bed, tea in its smooth cup — often not.
Most of the time she loves her neighbour, but never enough.
                          Is courage the answer?

          So she meets the gaze of
          the soon-to-be-quadriplegic man
          in mid-fall from the roof of his house; of

          her technician, mugged three days

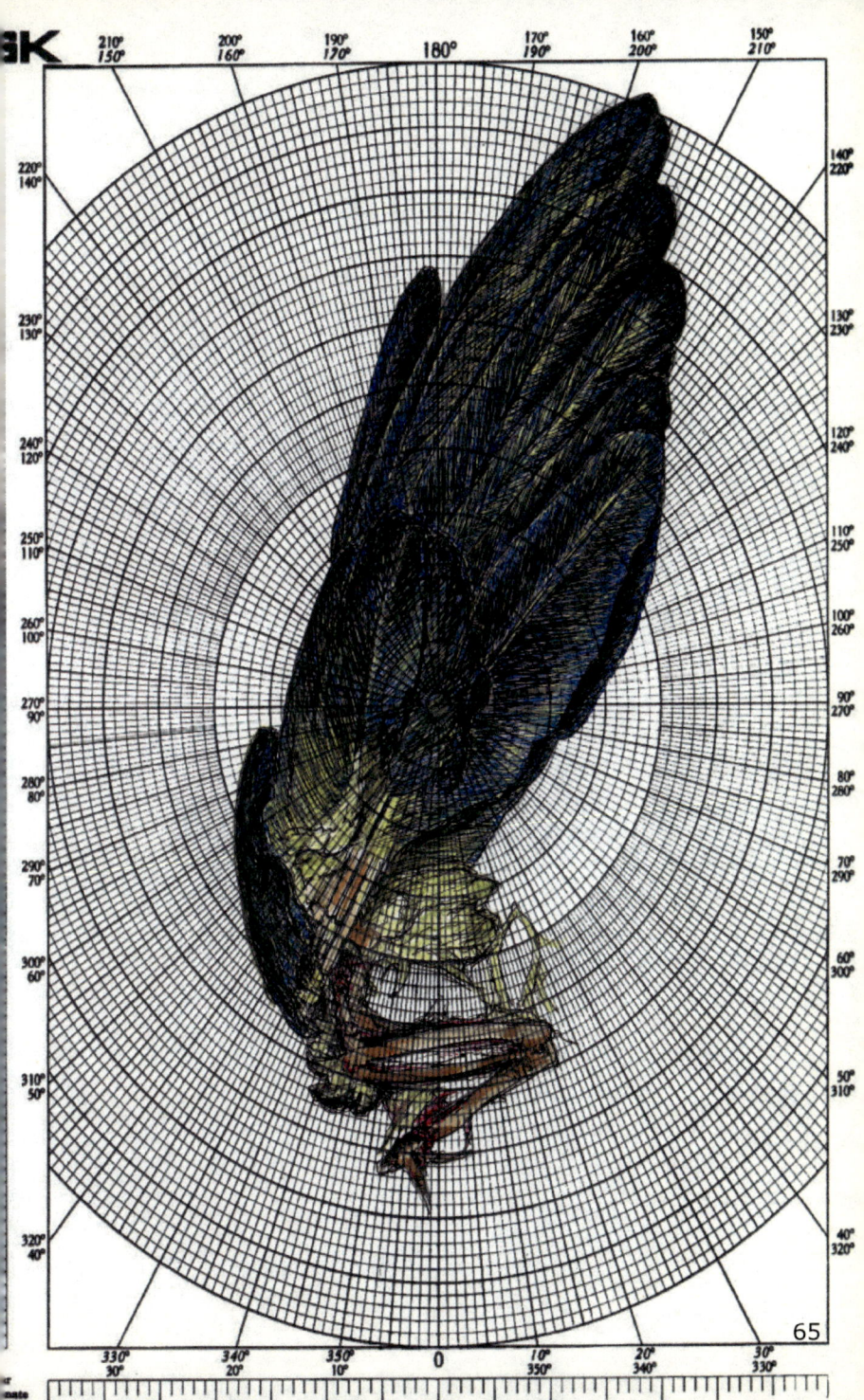

into retirement who recovers just enough
to be a stone on the surface of his family; of

the woman comatose in ITU, giving birth anyway,
whose husband will soon run off with babies,
house, and the nanny his firm brings in to help; of

ancient, mumbling Dorothy,
tumbling forward into the barn of her blouse

day after unused day.

            They all outstare her.

Then she looks through the lens of whatever variation
on breathing - stridor, stertor, Cheyne-Stokes -
her own last three moments turn out to be
and these fears turns out to be human.
Much harder's the everyday vertigo
as each second drops sheer to the next.

By now she'd try anything. Give a bottle of rum
to a sailor and one glass down the world free floats.
How she loves this milk-and-honey half-hour, a submariner
loosed into swirling air, who doesn't know or care
which way is up. Is that safety? Someone screams
                         Let go

and she's immersed in lukewarm water,
clinging to the ladder at the back of a boat
she doesn't know the name of,
just because the blues made her want to.
                         Let go

and because the others are laughing, buoyant,
and because the water's so intoxicatingly turquoise, she does,
circles, smiles for the camera (her eyes to that bottom rung)
and her face is still smiling when her hand grabs hold again,
even though her feet are not yet safe.

So what colours do they see, the buoyant ones?
Why don't they talk about it? Have her friends
found a way to dream lightly with brave feet
or are they, too, heavy machines, close-stacked
and shimmering with heat and gases but unable
to lift into the edgy atmospheres of sleep?

Which reminds her, friends have been lost
and need replacing, otherwise who will be there
at the end of the universe? Who will know what to do?

Colour is fugitive, and with a dark cloud,
the sea's an ink in which all measurements dissolve,
all boundaries fall to a rip of dread that kick-starts
the no-beginning, cracks the expanding edges,
rocks the great, sparse, space clock
till her feet are distraught fins, her fingers
colourless wings that will never look down again.

Fear, not light, becomes proof a thing exists.

NEPTUNE

Max distance from sun	4537
Min distance from sun	4456
	(millions of km)
Orbital period (earth years)	164.8
Rotation period	16h 7m
Orbital inclination	1.8°
Axial inclination	28.8°
Mass (earth = 1)	17.2
Volume (earth = 1)	57
Density (water = 1)	1.77
Surface gravity (earth = 1)	1.2
Average surface temp.	-200 °C
Albedo (fraction of light it reflects)	0.41
Equatorial diameter	50,538 km
Number of moons	13

~ i.e. a frozen gas ball
with 1,500 mph winds (a 220mph
hurricane is the fastest recorded on
earth —

Neptune

Her mother waits to give birth,
holds her stomach, moans, scratches, smiles.
Nowadays she's a fish, puffed up with a small mouth,
staring ahead or stumbling, on good days grumbling
or when her hand is taken, tugging behind like a balloon.

Who is this daughter who is the mother
who tried to do it right but got it all wrong?
Natural confusions when a year
equals two human lifetimes, when lifelines
chase each other round an icy world
and take it in turns to be furthest from the sun.

Unsettling, how weightless her mother seems —
fruit skin, food sac, eggshell, shucked off
Mermaid's Purse, how she floats, suspicious, but safe
there as anywhere. Surely she will deliver soon.

Pluto

Soon she'll honour another friend here
though he'll find no warmth this far from the sun
where the weather itself freezes
and in winter, falls to the ground.
If her house had a garden she'd plant a tree
but it hasn't so she'll bring him out here instead.

Will there be enough room?
Already the dead bicker among themselves, tell lies.
Each one of them's a thief and Steve, too, will cheat her,
slip episodes of her into some pocket deeper than his tumour
so she'll only find what's missing when he's gone.
That meal at his place? Mushrooms on Stanton Moor?
Some other knick-knack he's smuggled out
and stashed on a high shelf her memory can't reach?

Already there's no-one alive who has the full picture
and some of her most important stories
no longer have a witness, though there's freedom in that.

Cold wars are reciprocal and who knows, so far out,
what depths of her lie in wait, subtle and barbaric?
When friends have tried to sneak away without telling her
she's found out, glad to have memorised whole pages in case.
Ghost stories. What are the proper responsibilities
to the dead? She's stopped listening.

Even so, whenever there are decisions to be made,
Pluto tugs from the edges, only detectable
under extreme conditions and hard to put words to,
but swaying things with such a rush of gratitude and confusion,
she's left feeling lighter, lonelier, more private.

PLUTO

Max distance from sun	7375
Min distance from sun	4425
	(millions of km)
Orbital period (earth years)	247.7
Rotation period	6d 9h 17s
Orbital inclination	17.15°
Axial inclination	122.5°
Mass (earth = 1)	0.002
Volume (earth = 1)	0.01
Density (water = 1)	2.02
Surface gravity (earth = 1)	0.06
Average surface temp.	-225°C
Albedo (fraction of light it reflects)	0.6
Equatorial diameter	2,324 km
Number of moons	1

NB – it periodically slides
inside the orbit of Neptune
so these two planets are
alternately farthest from the sun

Undelivered return to HMRC Accounts Office

[unreadable] BY, West Yorkshire, BD98 8AA. GREAT BRITAIN

REVENUE & CUSTOMS
PRIVATE
ENV 153P (PPI)

W4Z 5058 (CMA)S

Advanced Mail
Second Class
AAAA-BAZR-HLZC

The Oort Cloud

Her father waits on an asteroid
halfway to the nearest known star
and in constant danger from 200 billion stones
that circle without purpose or meaning.

For thirty years she's longed to rescue him,
to draw him back against the solar tides.

It won't be long before her mother
makes her own attempt but by then
she will have built better arguments,
powered up a boat to swoosh and curve
her father home on a wall of spray, or rock or ice.

She'll tuck him up in bed
with a cup of tea, dry and warm,
to make up for being poorly,
just the two of them talking things over,
like the night she had German measles
and her brother was born.

1 Astronomical Unit = the distance from earth to the sun

$$= 93 \text{ million miles.}$$

THE OORT CLOUD

Distance from sun   20,000-100,000 AU

Little or no observational data, too far away.
Spherical, not disc shaped.
If it exists it must lose and gain objects but we don't know how.
Composed of trillions of lumps of rock and ice and dust.

Eris is larger than Pluto hence astronomers had to re-examine the definition of a planet & demote Pluto → dwarf planet

Eris

This far out, there's a peripheral logic
where planets are made or unmade.
Names change and any crux against which
measurements might be checked has all but gone out.
Hardly surprising her reason plays tricks:

suppose it's rays from her own eyes travelling out
to strike upon the world, that Pythagoras
was right, the eye as a candle, scattering beams.
And suppose it's her tail lights that stain the sunset
as she drives east, those reds reflected back
from the scalding mirror of the sun, overtaking her
and turning every fence post on the road ahead
so intricate and entire, she never notices the distance;

or suppose ray diagrams translate into dotted lines
along which stars jump closer, so it's possible
to see twenty-two million light years unaided;

and what if the widescreen–eye detects only edges
and movement which the mind in–fills at speed.
Thus idea leapfrogs on idea and crowds into busier,
blacker cities, where the tree in the precinct
fills with nuthatches at four o' clock and translates
to a twilit chatter of wings or leaves;

then imagine the quivering surface of her actions
is what she truly is, that there is no deeper self,
and all her noisy jealousies, good intentions, sly dependencies,
their jostlings in her heart, her head, don't matter.
What counts is the tally of leaves and wings.
Well it's a theory, and just in case, she tries to *act*
as she wants to *be*, like someone who has found
the secret of shooting golds and being cheerful.
All truth, all illusion, she strings her bow and grins;

but suppose nothing connects, and what's caught
in the flashes – owl pellets in the barn, a dancer, slowly,
in a damp room – are vents in the darkness.
All else becomes after-image of after-image, tricks
played by eyes clever enough to make darkness visible.

Then cygnets stretch their necks toward high ground
where the fuzzy ghost of her is snagged in thistledown,
that thin, against great standing waves of living and dying.
The eyes of sheep hold no prophecy
but give back the future as an open space
where the gale roars at her face, dislodges her.
She travels cold and fast, rides the tip
of the hairline crack where it rips into the unknown.
She's strident, shrill, trying her utmost with the fullness, the fury,
doing her best with the griefs, because they are intimately hers,
and giving every mountain, every tree, every river she has
to the work of slipping through.

ERIS (UB313)

Discovered	2003

The largest known dwarf planet, in the Kuiper belt
beyond Neptune.
At 10 billion miles from the sun and three times
further away than Pluto it is the most distant object
ever seen in orbit round the sun.

Surface temp	-405F
Diameter	2,400 km

Atmosphere is frozen methane — probably only a
few inches thick.

Moons	1, Dysnomia

Eris is the goddess of warfare and strife.

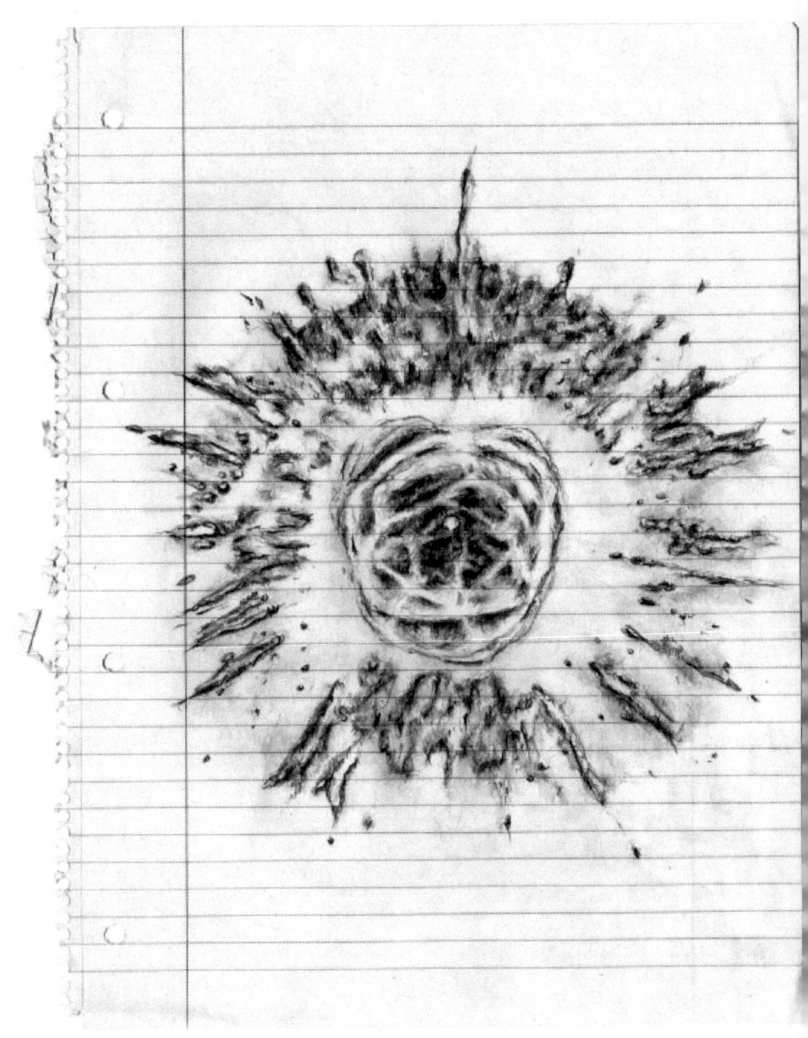

cafetería **horizonte**

C/. CERVANTES (MALAGUETA)
TELF.: 95-222 56 23 MÁLAGA

Nombre Sr Smith
Name

Empresa
Company

Teléfono Hotel 325　**Fax**
Phone

☐ **Ha llamado**　　　　☐ **Ha venido a visitarle**
　Telephoned　　　　　　　Come to see you

☐ **Volverá a llamar**　☐ **Desea verle**
　Will call again　　　　　Want to see you

☐ **Devuelva la llamada**　☐ **Urgente**
　Please, call him　　　　　Urgent

81

SUN

Distance from earth	149,600,000 km
Rotation period	27 days
	(as seen from earth)
Surface temp	5,500 °C
Core temp	15.6million °C
Mass	1 million earths
Diameter	1 million km
Solar cycle	22yrs
Energy output	386 billion billion
	megawatts

Solar cycle = magnetic cycles that cause N & S poles to swap.

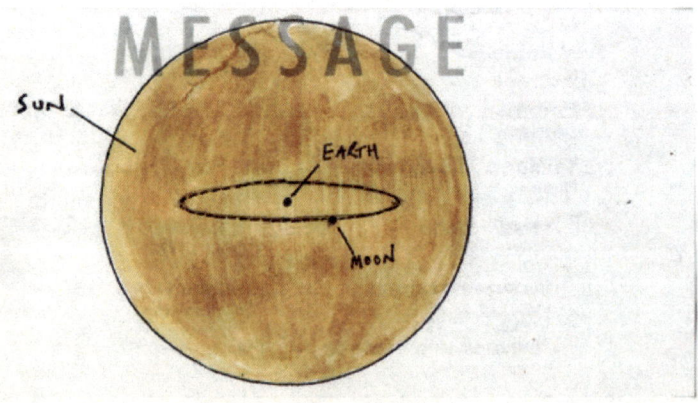

The Sun

Light is all we have, says the cosmologist,
gives us all we can ever know,
and what he can get from starlight's
enough to make anyone falsetto with excitement.

And nothing beats looking at the buzzing voltages
of your own star, its ions already hoping for a mineral home
and leaping toward the channels in her bones.
Thus light begins its journey through the self.

Her skin's become a fiery loam with sprays of force
and she's irresolute but her nerves have made their petition,
knowing from before birth where to grow to.
The shape of everything is starting to fit.
Only time is brighter than this.

Here, then, is where she sets the indivisible point of her
and does, without effort or question or doubt,
what is absolutely right for the moment.

Now, if only now,
the last piece of sky slots in, with everything
she has been or become, blazing and present.

8 Tuesday
Week 32 · 220-14

Universe as a whole Tint moving
in any particular direction OR IS
moving in all directions at once!

10h

200

8h

LYNX

7h

VI
M

6h

AURIGA
Capella

CAMELOPARDALIS

5h

PERSEUS

4h

Andromeda = 2.2 million
3h

light years away —
farthest we can see with the naked
eye from Northern Ireland

July				
M 31	3	10	17	24
T	4	11	18	25
W	5	12	19	26
T	6	13	20	27
F	7	14	21	28
S	1	8	15	22	29
S	2	9	16	23	30

August				
M	7	14	21	28
T	1	8	15	22	29
W	2	9	16	23	30
T	3	10	17	24	31
F	4	11	18	25
S	5	12	19	26	A
S	6	13	20	27

1h

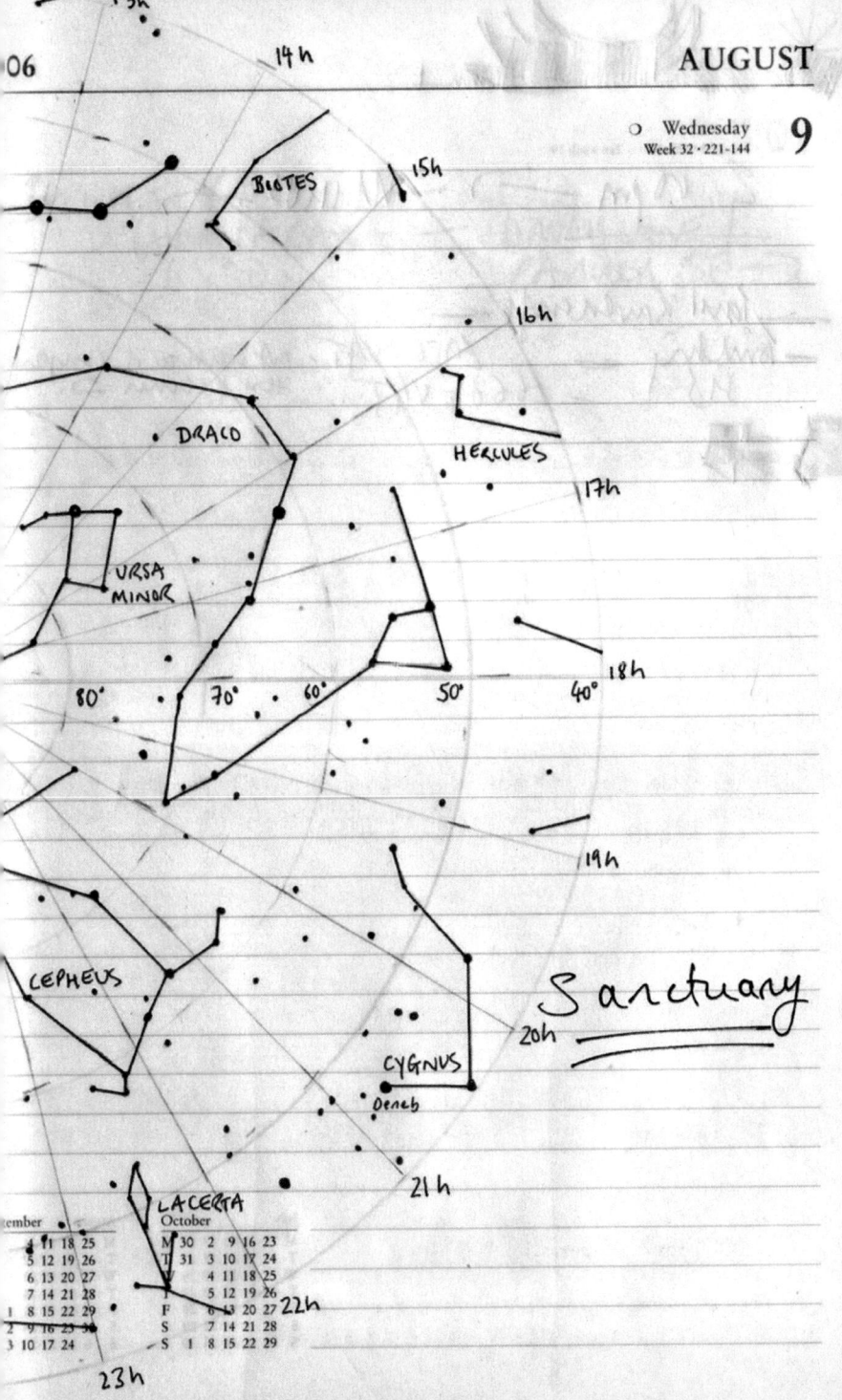

13h

14h

15h

BOÖTES

16h

DRACO

HERCULES

17h

URSA MINOR

18h

80°   70°   60°   50°   40°

19h

CEPHEUS

Sanctuary

20h

CYGNUS

Deneb

21h

LACERTA
October

22h

23h

List of Works

All images by Laura Daly, copyright © 2007-09, unless stated otherwise.

Cover artwork (also pp86&87): Map of North Celestial Pole with diary notes by Diana Syder superimposed on pages. Pencil and ink pen on paper, 21x29.1cm.

ppv&vi: Celestial Orbe Postcard using Leonard & Thomas Digge's drawing of an infinite Copernican universe (from 'A Perfit Description of the Caelestial Orbes', Prognostication Everlasting, 1576) Digital print on postcard, 8.9x13.9cm.

ppvii&viii: Drawings based on a sixteenth century medieval woodcut. Ink pen on paper, 14.8x10cm.

pp5&6: Bay of Rainbows, the Moon. Ink pen on paper, 18.3x16.4cm.

pp7&8: Nebula diffuse gas clouds. Pencil and ink pen on paper, 22.7x17.4cm.

pp9&10: Albrecht Berblinger (Tailor of Ulm) flying machine (front), Otto Lillianthal flying machine (reverse). Pencil, ink pen and felt tip on paper, 21x12cm.

pp11&12: Drawing based on 'Young Woman Fanning a Fire with a Bird's Wing', Martin Schongauer 1469. Pencil, felt tip and ink pen on Post It Note, 7.6x7.6cm.

pp13&14: Feather with notes written by Diana Syder superimposed on the reverse. Ink pen on polar graph paper, 21x29.6cm.

pp15&16: Diagrams of a human arm, the wing of the Wright brothers plane and a bird wing. Pencil and ink pen on 3 bird show tickets, 9.9x5.5cm.

pp17-20: Juvenile falcon wing with planet statistics by Syder superimposed on reverse. Silver ink & pencil on paper, 22.8x32cm.

p21: The shape and trajectories of orbits. Ink pen on paper. 14.5 x 21cm

pp23&24: Mercury. Pencil, biro, ink pen and felt tip on paper, 23 x32cm. Note written by Syder superimposed on the reverse.

pp25&26: Honey Buzzards. Ink pen on Zepellin Museum ticket, 6x15.2cm.

pp27&28: Venus. Biro, felt tip and ink pen on paper, 21.2x20.3cm.

pp30&31: Kepler's Law with diary notes by Diana Syder superimposed on pages. Pencil and ink pen on paper, 17.1x16cm.

pp32&33: The refraction of lenses - light rays and focus points, with diary notes. Pencil and ink pen on paper, 17.1x16cm.

pp35&36: Janter Manter Observatory. Ink pen, pencil and felt tip on paper, 11.5x22.2cm.

pp37&38: Buzz Aldrin's bootprint on the Moon. Biro, pencil and ink pen on paper, 20.5x23cm.

pp39-42: The Bay of Rainbows, the Moon. Pencil and ink pen on paper, 32.3x22.9cm.

pp43-46: 360 view of Mars viewed by NASA's Spirit Rover. Pencil, ink pen, acrylic and coloured pencil on card, 27.3x16.2cm.

pp47&48: Jupiter. Pencil and ink pen on card, 8.5x5.3cm.

p49: Drawing of spacecraft based on Franz Abdon Ulinski's Solar Energy Powered Rocket, 1927 (from Willy Leys 'Die Moglichkeit der Weltraumfahrt' (The Feasibility of Interplanetary Travel, 1928). Pencil and ink pen on paper, 15.2x10.2cm.

p50&51: Light wave propagation, with diary notes. Pencil and ink pen on paper, 17.1x16cm.

p53&54: The transit of Uranus. Pencil and ink pen on paper, 24.1x17.4cm.

pp57&58: Saturn's rings. Pencil and acrylic paint on paper, 22.8x34.7cm.

pp61&62: Saturn's rings. Pencil and ink pen on paper, 32.2x24.2cm.

pp63: Prescription and cancer screening appointment with information.

pp65&66: Broken pigeon wing. Pencil, biro, ink pen and felt tip on polar graph paper, 29.6x21cm.

pp71&72: Pluto. Pencil, ink pen and felt tip on paper, 10.5x14.8cm.

pp73&74: Fireballs. Based on the illustrations of Johann Esias Silberschlags theory of the July 23 1762 appearance of a fireball. Pencil and ink pen on paper, 13.2x23.5cm.

pp79&80: Nebula NGC 2392 (Eskimo Nebula). Pencil on paper, 22.6x29.4cm.

p80: Coaster, 9cm diameter.

p81&82pp91&92: The size of the Earth - Moon system in relation to the Sun. Pencil, ink pen and felt tip on paper, 13.9x6.8cm.

pp83&84: Solar prominence. Pencil, ink pen, biro, felt tip and oil